WORLD BOOK'S
LIBRARY OF NATURAL DISASTERS

THUNDERSTORMS

WORLD
BOOK

a Scott Fetzer company
Chicago
www.worldbookonline.com

World Book, Inc.
233 N. Michigan Avenue
Chicago, IL 60601
U.S.A.

For information about other World Book publications, visit our Web site at
http://www.worldbookonline.com or call **1-800-WORLDBK (967-5325)**.

For information about sales to schools and libraries, call **1-800-975-3250 (United States);
1-800-837-5365 (Canada)**.

2008 revised printing

Library of Congress Cataloging-in-Publication Data

Thunderstorms.
        p. cm. -- (World Book's library of natural disasters)
    Summary: "A discussion of major types of natural
disasters, including descriptions of some of the most
destructive; explanations of these phenomena, what
causes them, and where they occur; and information
about how to prepare for and survive these forces of
nature. Features include an activity, glossary, list of
resources, and index"--Provided by publisher.
    Includes bibliographical references and index.
    ISBN 978-0-7166-9812-8
    1. Thunderstorms--Juvenile literature.
I. World Book, Inc.
QC968.2.T58 2007
551.55'4--dc22
                              2007006674

World Book's Library of Natural Disasters
Set ISBN: 978-0-7166-9801-2

Printed in China
2 3 4 5 6 12 11 10 09 08

Editor in Chief: Paul A. Kobasa

Supplementary Publications
    Associate Director: Scott Thomas
    Managing Editor: Barbara A. Mayes

Editors: Jeff De La Rosa, Nicholas Kilzer,
    Christine Sullivan, Kristina A. Vaicikonis,
    Marty Zwikel

Researchers: Cheryl Graham, Jacqueline Jasek

Manager, Editorial Operations
    (Rights & Permissions): Loranne K. Shields

Graphics and Design
    Associate Director: Sandra M. Dyrlund
    Associate Manager, Design: Brenda B. Tropinski
    Associate Manager, Photography: Tom Evans
    Designer: Matt Carrington

Product development: Arcturus Publishing Limited
Writer: Jen Green
Editors: Nicola Barber, Alex Woolf
Designer: Jane Hawkins
Illustrator: Stefan Chabluk

Acknowledgments:

Christopher Godfrey: 33.

Corbis: 16 (Firefly Productions), 17 (Corbis), 18 (Jonathan Blair), 19 (Raymond Gehman), 21 (Martin Allen/ Sygma),
    22 (NASA), 23, 31 (Bettmann), 24 (Annie Griffiths Belt), 32 (Jim Reed), 38 (Soeren Steffen/ epa), 39 left,
    40 (Hulton-Deutsch Collection), 39 right (Toby Melville/ Reuters), 41 (Skyscan), 43 (John Heseltine).

FLPA: 12 (Jim Reed), 37 (B. Borrell Casals).

NASA/Goddard Space Flight Center Scientific Visualization Studio: 26.

Oxford Scientific: 11 bottom (Phototake Inc).

Science Photo Library: 6 (NASA), 8 (Mike Hollingshead/ Jim Reed Photography), 9, 14 (John A Ey III), 11 top,
    28 (Jim Reed), 15 (Sheila Terry), 20 (Pekka Parviainen), 25 (National Center for Atmospheric Research),
    27 (Quilla Ulmer/ Jim Reed Photography), 35 (David R. Frazier), 36 (Mike Agliolo), 42 (NRSC Ltd).

Shutterstock: cover/ title page, 4 (Jhaz Photography), 5 (Condor 36).

TABLE OF CONTENTS

Glossary There is a glossary of terms on pages 45-46. Terms defined in the glossary are in type **that looks like this** on their first appearance on any spread (two facing pages).

Additional resources Books for further reading and recommended Web sites are listed on page 47. Because of the nature of the Internet, some Web site addresses may have changed since publication. The publisher has no responsibility for any such changes or for the content of cited sources.

WHAT ARE THUNDERSTORMS?

A dazzling flash of lightning streaks across a stormy sky, followed by a deafening clap of thunder. This awesome display of nature's power is a thunderstorm. Thunderstorms release large amounts of energy in the form of thunder and lightning. They often bring fierce, gusting winds and downpours of rain, **hail,** or even snow.

Destructive power

Thunderstorms are the most common form of violent weather on Earth. About 45,000 thunderstorms occur throughout the world each day, adding up to more than 16 million storms each year. Most thunderstorms are small storms that last less than an hour and do little damage. However, even a small thunderstorm contains energy equal to that of a nuclear explosion. The most severe thunderstorms have 100 times as much energy.

Thunderstorms can cause massive destruction. They can send trees crashing onto buildings or cars, spark fires that destroy forests, and cause citywide power outages. Every year, thunderstorms kill hundreds of people around the world and lead to many more injuries.

Lightning streaks between a thundercloud and the ground during a violent thunderstorm.

Myth and mystery

Until the mid-1700's, thunderstorms were a great mystery. Many people believed that the gods used lightning as a weapon to show their anger. For example, the ancient Romans believed that their most powerful god, Jupiter, expressed his fury by hurling thunderbolts at anyone who offended him. In medieval Scandinavia, people believed that lightning flashed when their storm god, Thor, threw his mighty hammer. Some cultures thought places struck by lightning were sacred; other peoples considered them cursed. Even today, thunderstorms remain mysterious because scientists do not fully understand how they work.

THUNDERCLOUDS

The storm clouds that produce thunder and lightning are called **cumulonimbus** *(KYOO myuh loh NIHM buhs)* **clouds.** These clouds may reach great heights, towering up to 60,000 feet (18,000 meters) tall. Like all clouds, they consist of ice particles or water droplets and contain powerful **air currents.** Cumulonimbus clouds often have wide, flat tops, which makes them resemble giant anvils. For this reason, they are sometimes called "anvil clouds."

Towering cumulonimbus clouds can reach 60,000 feet (18,000 meters) into the sky.

WHEN AND WHERE DO THUNDERSTORMS DEVELOP?

Thunderstorms can strike anywhere on Earth, but they usually develop in locations with warm, **humid** weather. As a result, they occur most commonly in the **tropics,** regions around the **equator.** In many areas of Central Africa, Southeast Asia, and northern South America, thunderstorms happen more than 100 days each year.

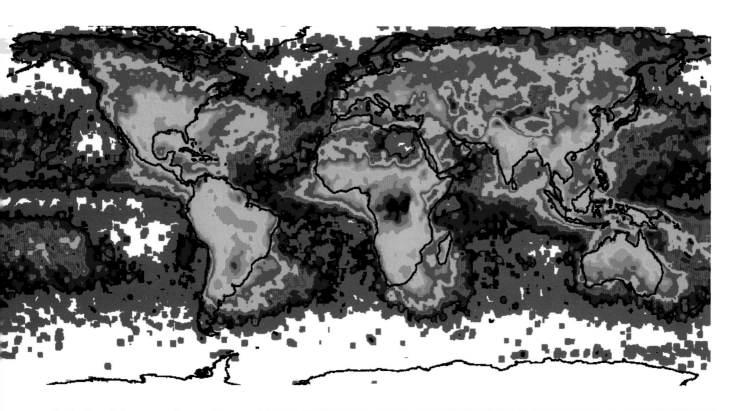

A National Aeronautics and Space Administration map, based on satellite images, reveals the frequency of lightning strikes throughout the world. Regions with the greatest frequency are shaded red and orange. Yellow, green, blue, purple, gray, and white (in that order) indicate decreasing frequency.

THE PLACES ON EARTH WITH THE MOST THUNDER

Tororo, in Uganda, East Africa, holds the record for the greatest number of thunderstorms per year. Tororo experienced thunder an average of 251 days a year during the 10-year period between 1967 and 1976. The town of Bogor, on the island of Java, Indonesia, is another location that commonly experiences thunderstorms. In the United States, thunderstorms occur most commonly in the Southeast, particularly in Florida.

Thunderstorms also occur commonly in **temperate** parts of the world, especially during the summer. In these areas, storms often break in the late afternoon or evening, after the heat of the day has built up. Thunderstorms occur much less frequently in such cold or dry areas as the **polar** regions or deserts.

Why do thunderstorms form?

Thunderstorms are powered by energy from the sun. All weather on Earth is caused by the sun's uneven heating of the planet's **atmosphere.** As the sun heats some parts of the atmosphere, the warm, lighter air in those regions rises, creating a zone of low **atmospheric pressure.** Cool air rushes in, replacing the air that has risen and producing winds. Such winds then carry all kinds of weather, from sunshine to rain, **hail,** and snow.

Thunderclouds need moisture and warm, rising air to develop. In sunny weather, the sun's **radiation** warms the ground, which, in turn, heats air near the surface of Earth. The sun also **evaporates** water from the surface of seas and lakes and from wet ground. The warm air rises, taking the **water vapor** with it. As the air rises, it cools, and the water vapor **condenses** to form clouds.

Thunderclouds can also develop in **weather systems** called **fronts,** where winds blow warm and cold **air masses** together, and in mountainous regions, where warm, moist air is forced upward by mountain slopes. Inside a towering thundercloud, the warm air rises rapidly, then cools at the top of the cloud and sinks down again. This process creates powerful vertical **air currents** called **updrafts** and **downdrafts.**

Moist, warm air rises as it meets a mountain. As the air cools, its moisture condenses to form clouds.

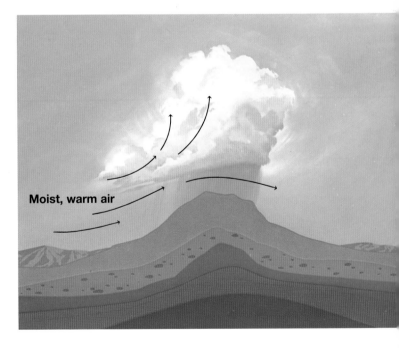

Moist, warm air

WHAT HAPPENS DURING A THUNDERSTORM?

Most thunderstorms are small, local storms that usually affect areas of about 10 square miles (25 square kilometers). They cause such limited damage as power outages and a few downed trees. However, some extremely powerful thunderstorms can flood entire towns.

Supercells

Large, long-lasting thunderstorms are called **supercells.** These severe storms feature strong winds and huge **cumulonimbus clouds.** Supercells release torrents of rain that can cause flooding. They may also produce devastating hailstorms. Some supercells create many violent **tornadoes.**

A supercell thunderstorm forms over Nebraska, producing torrential rain and at least two tornadoes.

How do clouds become electrically charged?

During a thunderstorm, **electrical** energy is released from clouds in the form of lightning. Scientists do not completely understand how electric charges build up inside thunderclouds. But many researchers believe this happens through a process called **charge separation.**

Like other clouds, thunderclouds consist of masses of tiny water droplets, ice crystals, and hailstones. As strong winds carry water droplets and ice crystals upward inside the cloud, the particles collide with heavier **hail** that is falling. These collisions make tiny electrically charged particles called **electrons** jump from **atoms** in the rising ice and water to the falling hail. The rising ice and water develops a positive charge; the falling hail becomes negatively charged. As a result, the top of the cloud becomes positively charged, and the bottom becomes negatively charged. Positive and negative charges attract each other. Eventually, the charge becomes so powerful that an electric spark surges from one part of the cloud to another. The flow of electrical energy produces a dazzling flash of lightning.

TRAPPED INSIDE A THUNDERCLOUD

In 1959, a U.S. Air Force pilot named William H. Rankin experienced firsthand the energy inside a thundercloud. On a flight across the eastern United States, Rankin had climbed to an altitude of 46,000 feet (14,000 meters) to avoid a thunderstorm when the engine of his airplane failed. He was forced to eject, dropping straight into a thundercloud. Rankin's parachute opened, but he was shot up, then down, then flipped over and over by violent **air currents.** He spent a total of 40 minutes inside the thundercloud, battered by wind, rain, and hail, before crash landing in a tree. Rankin survived the ordeal, but he was covered with cuts and bruises.

A bolt of lightning streaks between a cumulonimbus stormcloud and the ground. Lightning also causes the cloud to glow from within.

THE FORT WORTH HAILSTORM

Every year, thunderstorms cause billions of dollars of damage throughout the world. Hailstorms rank among the most violent and destructive of these storms. On May 5, 1995, a severe hailstorm struck Fort Worth, Texas, causing over $1 billion in damage and injuring many people.

A gathering storm

The Fort Worth hailstorm occurred during the town's annual Mayfest celebrations. Large crowds had gathered to join in the celebrations, which included food, music, and a fair. The afternoon of May 5 was warm and **humid,** and a strong wind blew from the southeast—ideal conditions for a violent thunderstorm. Fort Worth lies at a junction of **weather systems** where three **air masses** often collide. A violent storm such as a **supercell** hits the town about once every 10 years.

Pelted by hailstones

In the early evening, the skies above Fort Worth blackened and a violent storm broke. Hailstones the size of baseballs hurtled down, scattering

Canada
United States
Mexico

Oklahoma

Arkansas

New Mexico

Air mass brings moisture from the land

Texas

Dallas

Fort Worth

Louisiana

Air mass brings moisture from the Pacific Ocean

Air mass brings moisture from the Gulf of Mexico

Mexico

200 Miles
200 Kilometers

Gulf of Mexico

Three air masses converge (come together) around Dallas and Fort Worth, Texas, on May 5, 1995. The weather system produced a hailstorm that resulted in over $1 billion in damage.

the crowds. The ice pellets shattered glass roofs and every skylight in the city hall. They punctured car roofs and smashed windshields, showering people inside with ice and glass. The hailstorm knocked more than 100 of the city's police cars out of action.

In addition to the hailstorm, the supercell produced localized flooding. In all, 14 people were either killed by **hail** or drowned. One person died after being struck by lightning. About 80 more people suffered serious injuries, including cuts and bruises caused by hailstones. Some experts estimated that the storm caused around $2 billion in damage to the Dallas and Fort Worth area, making it the most costly thunderstorm ever to strike the United States.

Hailstones, which can easily shatter windshields (right), make driving conditions extremely dangerous, especially at night (below).

AT RISK OF HAIL

In North America, hailstorms most often strike in a zone east of the Rocky Mountains that stretches from Alberta, Canada, through the Great Plains to Texas. A belt that runs through eastern Colorado, Nebraska, and Wyoming is known as "Hail Alley" due to the high frequency of hailstorms in the region. Cheyenne, Wyoming, is the town most often struck by hailstones. It experiences about 10 days of hail a year.

WHAT ARE LIGHTNING AND THUNDER?

The first scientific studies of lightning took place in the mid-1700's. In 1752, the American scientist and statesman Benjamin Franklin explained that lightning is an **electrical** effect. Franklin had flown a kite in a thunderstorm with a key tied to the end of the string. He reported that he saw sparks leaping from the key toward his hand. Franklin's experiment was very dangerous, and he could have been killed.

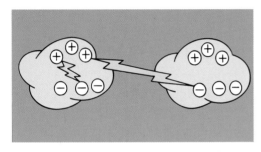

Lightning leaps within and between clouds (above) to equalize the electrical charges that have built up.

Cloud-to-air lightning (below) discharges during a supercell thunderstorm.

What is lightning?

Lightning is a giant electric spark in the sky caused by the flow of positive and negative electric charges toward one another. A flash of lightning may **discharge** about 100 million volts of electric potential. We often think of lightning as leaping from the clouds to the ground, but only one in five lightning strikes reaches the ground. Most lightning occurs in midair. When charges flow within a thundercloud, intracloud lightning occurs. Charges that leap from a cloud to the air cause cloud-to-air lightning. When charges flow between two clouds, they can produce cloud-to-cloud lightning.

Cloud-to-ground lightning

Most cloud-to-ground lightning occurs because the ground beneath a thundercloud develops a positive charge. As a result, **electrons** flow from the negatively charged base of the cloud to the ground. As the charges race downward, they take the shortest route to the ground, traveling through such tall objects as church spires or trees. That is why it is dangerous to take shelter under a tree during a storm.

Several leaders and strokes

A flash of lightning actually consists of several discharges called **leaders** and **strokes.** As the first spark descends from the cloud, it moves in a series of short bursts or steps with tiny pauses in between. For this reason, it is called a stepped leader. As it nears the ground, another leader rises from the ground to meet it. The two join to make a channel down which electricity flows. The first discharge is immediately followed by a very bright, upward-moving spark called the return stroke. The return stroke produces the light that we call lightning. As many as 20 other leaders and return strokes may follow along the path of the first stroke. But these events usually happen so quickly that we see just one dazzling flash.

THUNDER

As lightning streaks through the air, it heats the air in its path to more than 50,000 °F (28,000 °C). As a result, the air expands rapidly, producing a **shock wave.** This shock wave creates sound waves that we hear as a loud clap of thunder. The sound of thunder varies from a single, deafening crack to a low rumble. We always see lightning before we hear thunder because light travels faster than sound.

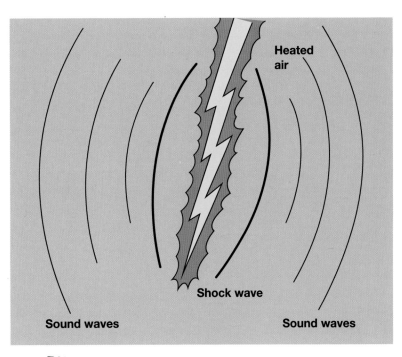

Lightning heats the air that it travels through, causing the gas to expand very rapidly. The resulting shock wave produces the sound waves of thunder.

TYPES OF LIGHTNING

Lightning may appear in several different shapes, but they all form by the same process. People have invented several terms to describes different forms of lightning.

Cloud-to-ground lightning often takes the shape of forked lightning that is split into many branches. Cloud-to-ground lightning may also appear as a single stream of zigzagging light known as streak lightning. When a lightning stroke is blown sideways by the wind, people may see parallel streaks called ribbon lightning. As lightning fades, it may break up into a string of individual lights known as bead or chain lightning. Sheet lightning may light up the whole sky or make clouds appear to glow from within. Heat lightning, which often appears on summer nights, is so far away that observers cannot hear its thunder.

Forked lightning splits into many branches as it travels between a cloud and the ground.

BALLS OF FIRE

Ball lightning is a very rare form of lightning. During storms, observers have seen glowing balls about the size of grapefruits entering buildings through open windows or chimneys. Ball lightning often hovers or drifts slowly and then explodes. In 1753, the Russian scientist Georg W. Richmann was killed by a ball of lightning while performing an experiment with an early **lightning conductor.** During a storm, lightning surged through Richmann's lightning rod. To his surprise, the rod produced a ball of light that floated toward him and struck him. It then exploded, and Richmann died instantly. The explosion knocked Richmann's assistant unconscious, but he survived.

St. Elmo's fire

One rare form of lightning known as **St. Elmo's fire** appears as a green, blue, or purplish glow flickering around such tall, pointed objects as church spires and ships' masts. The name *Elmo* comes from *Erasmus,* the name of a Christian saint who was believed to protect sailors. Scientists explain that the glow accompanies a steady discharge of electricity from certain objects. It occurs during thunderstorms or at other times when electrified clouds are present and is visible only in complete darkness. Today, St. Elmo's fire is sometimes seen around the propellors and wings of airplanes that are flying through electrified clouds.

For centuries, sailors have reported seeing the electrical phenomenon known as St. Elmo's fire glowing from the tops of ships' masts. The glow is produced by a steady discharge of electricity that occurs during thunderstorms or when electrified clouds are present.

AIRCRAFT AT RISK

Pilots may alter their aircraft's flight path to steer clear of thunderstorms, but they cannot always travel around or above large weather systems.

Thunderstorms pose a number of dangers to the aircraft industry. Airlines may delay flights partly to protect the ground crew from lightning strikes while they service the planes. Once in the air, aircraft may change course to avoid thunderclouds, but they cannot always avoid large storms. Aircraft in flight typically suffer little damage when struck by lightning. The plane's metal body is designed to **conduct** electric current so that the charge passes harmlessly over it. However, a small number of plane crashes are thought to have resulted from lightning strikes.

The Elkton disaster

On Dec. 8, 1963, a Pan American Airways 707 aircraft crashed at Elkton, Maryland, after being struck by lightning. The lightning spark penetrated a fuel tank in the wing and set the fuel vapor on fire. The aircraft burst into flames and fell to the ground. All 81 people on board died—the largest number of people ever killed by a single lightning strike.

Lightning has also damaged the vital electronic flight control equipment in some aircraft. After the Elkton crash, aircraft manufacturers took steps to ensure that fuel tanks and all essential equipment were fully protected against lightning.

Rain, hail, and turbulence

Thunderstorms hold other perils for aircraft besides lightning. During a severe storm, **hail** can damage an aircraft's engines or even crack the cockpit window. Torrential rain can cause the engines to fail. The powerful **air currents** within thunderclouds may cause a disturbance in the air known as **turbulence** that can make it difficult for pilots to control the aircraft. Several small planes are thought to have been torn apart during severe thunderstorms.

Onlookers survey the wreckage of the airship *Shenandoah,* which broke apart in a violent thunderstorm in 1925.

THE WRECK OF THE SHENANDOAH

In 1925, turbulence during a thunderstorm caused the destruction of the U.S. Navy airship *Shenandoah.* Such airships consist of small engines and a sealed cabin, called a gondola, suspended below a giant balloon filled with lighter-than-air gas. On Sept. 2, 1925, the *Shenandoah* flew into a thunderstorm that caused the flimsy craft to be jerked thousands of feet up and down until it broke into three pieces and crashed.

FOREST FIRES

Even a small thunderstorm can cause large-scale destruction if lightning starts a fire. Every year, fires sparked by lightning destroy thousands of acres of forest throughout the world. In time, forests grow back, but these fires can cause millions of dollars of damage in the short term.

"Dry lightning"

Forest fires occur most often during summer or after a **drought.** Warm, dry weather causes vegetation below trees to dry out. Forest fires may be started by "dry lightning," lightning that occurs when extremely dry weather **evaporates** rain during a thunderstorm before the rain hits the ground. When a fire is started under such conditions, there is no rain to dampen the flames.

Fire rages through the forests of Yellowstone National Park, Wyoming, in 1988.

The Yellowstone fires

In the United States, a devastating forest fire struck Yellowstone National Park, largely located in Wyoming, in 1988. The Yellowstone fires began on June 22, when lightning set a clump of pine trees

ablaze. At first, park authorities let the fires burn unchecked because of a park policy to allow fires to burn out naturally.

However, by July 22, fire had spread to many parts of the park. The authorities decided to try to stop the blaze. A total of 25,000 firefighters were brought in to quench the flames—at a cost of $140 million—but they did not succeed.

Fanned by strong winds, the Yellowstone fires raged uncontrollably through August. Over 150,000 acres (60,700 hectares) of forest were engulfed by flame in a single day. Snow finally dowsed the flames in the fall, but not before 36 percent of the entire park had burned. The fires also destroyed 67 buildings. Two firefighters and hundreds of animals died after becoming trapped by the flames.

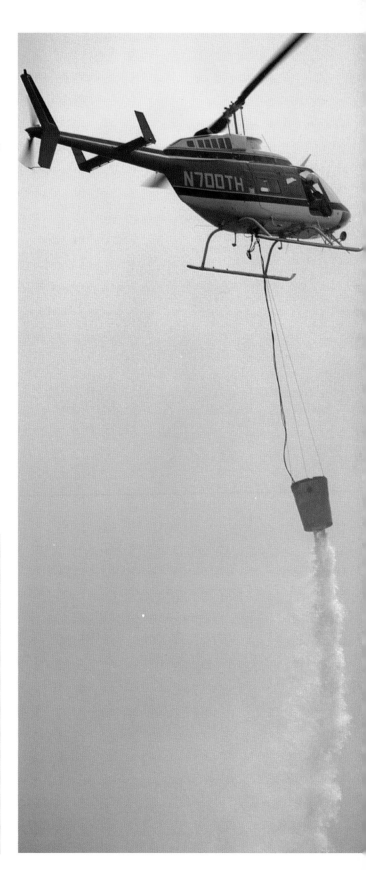

A helicopter dumps fire-dampening chemicals as part of an effort to quench a blaze in Yellowstone National Park in 1988.

FIGHTING FOREST FIRES

Firefighters use a variety of techniques to control forest fires. They use fire engines and helicopters to dump chemicals or water on the flames and to wet down vegetation. In the United States, Russia, and other countries, firefighters called smokejumpers drop by parachute to put out small fires before they develop into major blazes. When planting forests, foresters leave gaps called **firebreaks** between stands of trees to prevent fire from spreading. During major fires, these breaks are sometimes enlarged by digging ditches or by felling more trees to try to keep the fire from jumping across the gap.

Thunderstorms pose dangers from the tremendous amounts of water they release. Dark thunderclouds can suddenly produce torrential rain over a small area in an event called a **cloudburst.** A thunderstorm lasting only one or two hours can release up to 26 million gallons (100 million liters) of water. Regions hit by cloudbursts may receive a significant proportion of their annual rainfall in a matter of hours.

Floodwater

Small to moderate thunderstorms often bring welcome rain that provides essential water supplies for farms, industries, and cities. However, severe thunderstorms may produce heavy downpours that can lead to disastrous floods. Even small streams and gently flowing rivers can turn into raging torrents that uproot trees and sweep away houses and cars. If rivers burst their banks, the floodwater can sweep into buildings and destroy valuable crops.

A thundercloud drenches a localized area during a cloudburst in Finland.

Flash floods

Many of the most destructive floods caused by thunderstorms occur in hilly or mountainous regions. In steep terrain, water from heavy rain cascades down hillsides, causing rivers to rise quickly. The resulting surge of water, called a **flash flood,** allows little time for people to be warned of danger (see pages 22-23).

In 1992, the town of Vaison-la-Romaine in southern France was hit by floods following a cloudburst in nearby hills. The local river, the Ouvèze, quickly swelled into a raging torrent. A wall of water 50 feet (15 meters) high swept through the town, carrying away houses and vehicles and killing 38 people.

A torrent of muddy water roars through the streets of Vaison-la-Romaine, France, during a destructive flash flood in 1992.

A DOWNPOUR IN THE DESERT

Surprisingly, thunderstorms can be highly destructive in such normally dry places as deserts. The ground in these regions is usually too hard and dry to absorb heavy rain. As a result, water streams across the surface of the land, carrying soil and rocks. The town of Calama in Chile lies in one of the driest places on Earth—the Atacama Desert. Before 1972, no rain had fallen on Calama for 400 years. But on Feb. 10, 1972, a thunderstorm broke over the town, releasing torrential rainfall. The unexpected downpour caused flooding and **landslides.**

FLASH FLOOD IN THE ROCKIES

A satellite image shows a squall line developing over the Atlantic Ocean.

Flash floods occur mainly in mountainous regions, sometimes as a result of severe thunderstorms accompanied by sudden rises in wind called **squalls.** A line of thunderclouds known as a **squall line** can form where warm, **humid** air rises rapidly as it meets a slope, then cools and **condenses.** High in the mountains, the rain that falls during a squall is quickly channeled into narrow **gorges.** The water level in these rivers rises rapidly, allowing little chance for people downstream to be warned of the danger.

The Big Thompson River

In 1976, a flash flood devastated a 15-mile (24-kilometer) stretch of the Big Thompson River in Colorado. The Big Thompson River begins in the Rocky Mountains and flows eastward, dropping through a steep, narrow **canyon.** The wild scenery of this canyon makes it popular with hikers and campers. On July 31, 1976, more than 3,000 campers had gathered in the canyon to enjoy a vacation break.

The storm moves in

During the afternoon of July 31, clouds began to gather over the canyon. By 6:00 p.m., towering thunderclouds filled the sky and heavy rain began to fall. Such clouds normally drift on the wind, spreading their rainfall over a wide area. But the storm clouds above the Big Thompson canyon remained still. As much as 12 inches (30 centimeters) of rain fell in less than five hours.

A wall of water

Water levels in the river rose rapidly. As the bulge of water entered the canyon, the narrow walls blocked its flow. A wall of water around 20 feet (6 meters) high built up, then broke free and surged down the canyon at great speed. When it reached the campground, the water swept away trees, tents, and recreational vehicles. The water also washed away roads, bridges, and much of U.S. Highway 34, making it difficult for emergency services to reach the area. The flood destroyed more than 400 residences and 50 businesses and drowned 139 people.

FLASH FLOOD IN THE PYRENEES

In August 1996, a violent thunderstorm caused a disastrous flood in a remote part of the Pyrenees Mountains in northern Spain. A severe **cloudburst** high in the mountains produced hailstones the size of marbles and unleashed 3 inches (8 centimeters) of rain in less than two hours. The downpour triggered a flash flood that swept through a campsite in the valley below. The flood killed 87 people and injured 180 others.

A rescue worker searches for victims in the waters of the Big Thompson River near flooded U.S. Highway 34, after the flash flood of 1976.

HAILSTONES

Hailstones are lumps of ice that form inside thunderclouds. They can have round or irregular shapes. In the United States, thunderstorms most often produce **hail** in spring or early summer. When large hailstones rain down, they can injure or even kill people and animals, damage buildings and vehicles, and cause hundreds of millions of dollars of damage to crops.

A farmer surveys hail damage to his crop of sunflowers in North Dakota in 1985.

How do hailstones form?

Hailstones start as frozen raindrops or snow pellets called **hail embryos.** Powerful winds inside a thundercloud carry the hail embryos up and down within the cloud. At the base of the cloud, the embryos collide with **supercooled** water droplets, cold drops of water that remain liquid at temperatures below their **freezing point.**

The embryos become covered with a layer of moisture. **Air currents** may then carry the embryos upward, causing the moisture to freeze. This process may be repeated until some hailstones acquire up to 25 layers of ice. The hailstones become so heavy that they plummet to the ground.

If a hailstone is cut in two, it is possible to see alternate layers of clear and cloudy ice inside. The clear ice comes from the lower region of the cloud, where water freezes slowly. The cloudy ice comes from the upper region, where water freezes instantly. The number of layers indicates how many times the stone has whirled up and down inside the cloud.

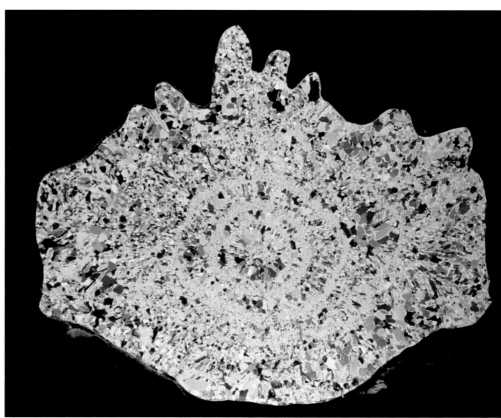

A cross-section of a hailstone reveals alternating layers of clear and cloudy ice, indicating the number of times it whirled up and down in a cloud. The hailstone, which was approximately the size of a grapefruit, fell in Kansas in 1970.

Hailstone sizes

Hailstones are generally larger than 0.2 inch (0.5 centimeter) in diameter and smaller than 1 inch (2.5 centimeters) in diameter. However, severe storms can produce pellets the size of golf balls or oranges, or even larger. Hailstones may fall at speeds of 22 miles (35 kilometers) per hour or more, making them icy missiles. Large hailstones can injure people and animals. A violent shower of hail can flatten a field of wheat, corn, or cotton in minutes. Every year, thunderstorms destroy about 1 percent of the world's crops.

STUDYING HAILSTONES

The Italian scientist Alessandro Volta (1745-1827) was one of the first people to study hailstones. Volta cut ice pellets in two and observed the layers inside. He rightly guessed that hailstones form around frozen raindrops or snowflakes.

DEADLY HAILSTORMS

Hailstorms are relatively common in **humid, temperate** parts of the world. They are less common in the **tropics** because **hail** that forms in these regions usually melts before it hits the ground. Hail-bearing clouds often develop near mountain ranges. As air rises over mountains, it contributes to powerful **updrafts** inside thunderclouds that produce hail. As a result, the region lying south of the Himalaya Mountains in southern Asia often experiences hailstorms.

Death in the mountains

Northern India and Bangladesh have a long history of violent hailstorms. Some historians believe that, in the A.D. 800's, a hailstorm killed more than 200 people at Roopkund Lake, high in the Himalaya in India. Some of the victims' bodies lay preserved

As air rises over the Himalaya, shown below in a computer-generated image from satellite photographs, the air contributes to updrafts inside thunderclouds that produce violent hailstorms across northern India and Bangladesh.

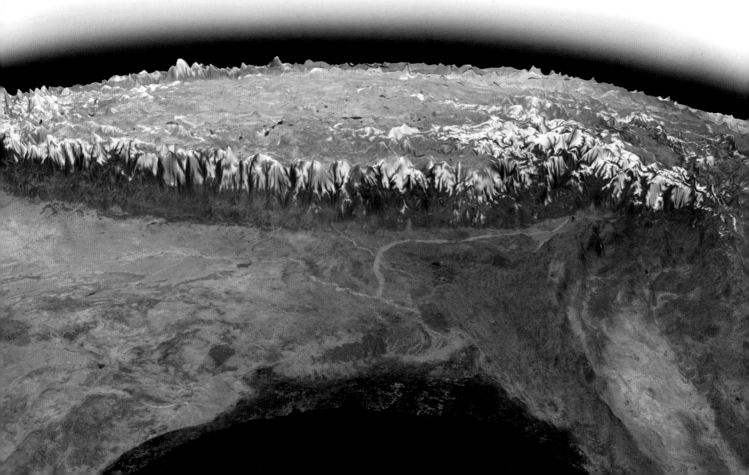

in ice. Their bodies have marks showing that they died from head wounds after being pelted by hailstones the size of baseballs.

In 1888, a severe storm hit the district of Moradabad in India. A shower of large hailstones destroyed crops and stripped leaves from the trees. A total of 246 people were killed by the hailstones, and 1,600 cattle also died. The Moradabad storm ranks as the world's deadliest hailstorm.

Almost a century after the Moradabad disaster, another terrible hailstorm struck south of the Himalaya. On April 14, 1986, hailstones the size of grapefruits rained down on the town of Gopalganj in Bangladesh, killing 92 people. The largest ice chunks weighed 2.3 pounds (1 kilogram). The Gopalganj hailstorm ranks as the world's heaviest hail shower.

THE HEAVIEST HAILSTONES

The largest hailstone ever recorded in the United States fell on Aurora, Nebraska, on June 22, 2003. It measured 7 inches (17.8 centimeters) across. Even larger chunks of ice, sometimes called **ice meteors,** have fallen in other countries. In 1959, a piece of ice weighing 4.2 pounds (1.9 kilograms) fell in Kazakhstan, in central Asia. In 1829, an ice meteor weighing 4.4 pounds (2 kilograms) dropped on Córdoba, Spain. Scientists do not know how these huge, and potentially lethal, chunks of ice form in the air.

A hailstone measuring 7 inches (17.8 centimeters) in diameter, the largest on record in the United States, fell on Aurora, Nebraska, in June 2003.

TORNADOES

A **tornado,** also known as a "twister," is a violent, whirling funnel of air that forms beneath a thundercloud. Tornadoes have structures similar to those of **hurricanes,** but tornadoes are much smaller and last for shorter time periods. Many tornadoes last for a few minutes and leave only a narrow trail of damage. However, the winds inside the most powerful tornadoes rank as the strongest winds on Earth, sometimes swirling at speeds greater than 300 miles (480 kilometers) per hour. As a severe tornado weaves across the landscape, it can leave a track of devastation measuring about 1 mile (1.6 kilometers) wide.

How do tornadoes form?

Most tornadoes develop from severe thunderstorms. Large, destructive tornadoes form during violent thunderstorms called **supercells.** These storms develop on warm, **humid** days when **air masses** blow into each other from opposite directions. As a mass of warm, humid air collides with cold air, the warm air rushes upward. When winds at higher levels have different speeds and directions than winds at lower elevations, the air may begin to spiral, becoming a rotating column of air called a **mesocyclone.** A dark, heavy cloud called a wall cloud forms beneath the mesocyclone. Funnel-shaped clouds develop from the wall cloud. When one of these funnels touches the ground, it becomes a tornado.

A tornado develops below a supercell thunderstorm in Nebraska in 2004.

The eye of the storm

The dark funnel of a tornado consists of powerful winds whirling around a central **eye.** The rapidly rising air creates a zone of low pressure in the eye. As a result, the tornado acts like a giant vacuum cleaner, sucking up everything in its path. Cars, trailers, and even trains may be picked up, hurled through the air, and smashed to the ground. Tornadoes can snap trees in half and rip down power lines. A powerful tornado can tear the roof off a house with such violence that the house appears to explode.

Tornadoes strike the Midwestern and Southern sections of the United States more often than any other region of the world.

A PLAYGROUND FOR TORNADOES

The United States experiences more tornadoes each year than does any country in the world. From 800 to 1,100 of these storms strike in the United States annually. Most tornadoes hit the Midwestern and Southern states during spring and summer. Fully 80 percent of the world's tornadoes touch down in a region known as Tornado Alley, which includes Texas, Oklahoma, Kansas, Nebraska, and Iowa. Australia ranks as the country with the second highest number of tornadoes each year.

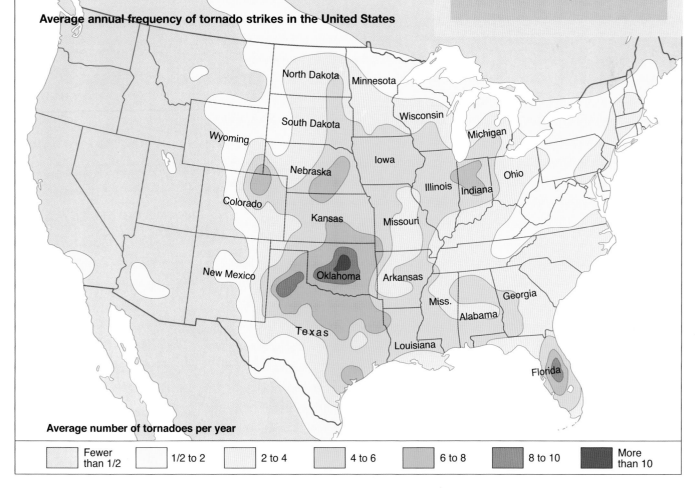

Average annual frequency of tornado strikes in the United States

Average number of tornadoes per year

| Fewer than 1/2 | 1/2 to 2 | 2 to 4 | 4 to 6 | 6 to 8 | 8 to 10 | More than 10 |

THE SUPER TORNADO OUTBREAK

Many of the most destructive **tornado** incidents involve a group of tornadoes, an event known as a **tornado outbreak.** On April 3 and 4, 1974, a total of 148 tornadoes ripped across 13 U.S. states and 1 Canadian province in an event known as the Super Tornado Outbreak. The tornadoes left devastation along a trail more than 2,500 miles (4,000 kilometers) long.

Early in the morning of April 3, **meteorologists** noticed a cold **air mass** blowing east from the Rocky Mountains toward Texas. In Texas, the mass collided with warm, **humid** air moving up from the Gulf of Mexico. The collision caused three separate **squall lines** to form, with thunderclouds towering to 60,000 feet (18,000 meters).

The first tornadoes began to form at around 2:00 p.m. They grew in number and intensity, with as many as 15 tornadoes raging in several different places at once by early evening. Severe storms continued through the night. Tornadoes touched down across a vast strip of land in the center of the United States, from Alabama and Georgia in the South to the Great Lakes in the North. Winds blew all the tornadoes northeast, causing them to leave parallel tracks of destruction.

All the tornadoes of the 1974 outbreak blew northeast, cutting parallel tracks through the Unites States and southern Canada.

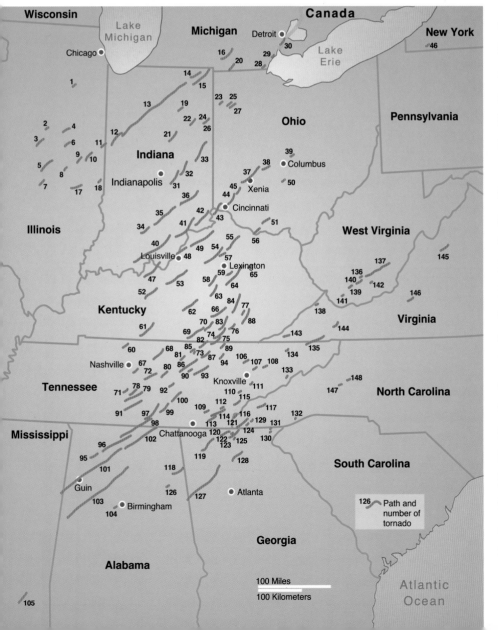

The damage

Of the outbreak's 148 tornadoes, meteorologists rated 6 as F5—the highest level on the Fujita scale, which measures the strength of tornadoes by the amount of damage they cause. Six towns were struck by two separate tornadoes.

The little town of Guin, Alabama, was completely destroyed. In nearby Jasper, the police station blew away. The outbreak ended at around 9:00 a.m. on April 4. Tornadoes had killed 330 people and injured more than 5,480 others. The Super Tornado Outbreak ranks as the largest tornado outbreak in U.S. history.

A tornado in the 1974 Super Tornado Outbreak tore the entire side from a house in Xenia, Ohio.

IN THE PATH OF A TORNADO

On April 3, 1974, the town of Xenia, Ohio, suffered a direct hit from an F5 tornado. Thirty-four people died, and 3,000 homes were destroyed. The tornado ripped off the top floor of the high school. It picked up a school bus and sent it crashing onto the school stage, where students had been rehearsing a play just moments earlier. A witness reported that the only sounds were the wind, crashes, and people praying.

MICROBURSTS

Microbursts are intense, localized downward blasts of air. Thunderstorms often cause these pockets of rapidly sinking cold air. As the blast hits the ground, it spreads in all directions, like water from a faucet hitting the sink. Microbursts can cause a sudden change in wind speed or direction known as **wind shear.**

Why do microbursts occur?

Rain, **hail,** or ice in a thundercloud can produce a region of rapidly sinking cold air. As the moisture **evaporates** or melts, it cools the air around it. As a result, a pocket of relatively heavy air sinks at high speed. If not all of the moisture has evaporated by the time the air blast reaches the ground, heavy rain may accompany the microburst. Microbursts occur over small areas less than 2½ miles (4 kilometers) across. However, they can produce winds gusting at up to 170 miles (270 kilometers) per hour.

A microburst pounds McPherson, Kansas, in 1997 with a very strong downward blast of cold air.

Microburst damage

People report more than a dozen microbursts in the United States every year. They are sometimes mistaken for **tornadoes** because microbursts can cause similar destruction. On July 15, 1995, a microburst struck Jefferson County in upstate New York. Winds gusting at 100 miles (160 kilometers) per hour flattened millions of trees, damaged buildings, and killed five people. That night, the United States closed its portion of the Thousand Islands suspension bridge that connects the United States and Canada due to the high winds.

Microbursts also pose dangers to such vehicles as aircraft (see pages 34-35) and ships. In May 1986, a violent microburst sank a ship called the *Pride of Baltimore* during a voyage in the Caribbean Sea.

DERECHOS

A **derecho** is a fast-moving storm with extremely powerful, gusting winds. Unlike the spiraling or chaotic winds in tornadoes or microbursts, the winds of a derecho blow in straight lines. *Derecho* is a Spanish word meaning *straight ahead*. Derechos can strike without warning, usually during hot, **humid** summer nights. The enormous gusts travel as fast as 90 miles (150 kilometers) per hour and leave a storm track hundreds of miles long. On July 4, 1999, a derecho raged across North Dakota, Minnesota, southern Canada, and Maine, felling 25 million trees.

A derecho races southward—from right to left—across Kansas, laden with dust and sand.

A HAZARD TO AIRCRAFT

Microbursts can damage forests, power lines, buildings, ships, and bridges. But they pose their greatest risk to aircraft, especially during takeoff and landing. These unpredictable, powerful gusts of wind are thought to be one of the main causes of plane crashes.

What happens to an airplane during a microburst?

An airplane heading into a microburst experiences a sudden **headwind**—a wind blowing straight toward the aircraft. As a result, airflow increases over the wings, causing the plane to rise. However, as the craft passes through the microburst, it hits a

An airplane rises and falls as it experiences a headwind and tailwind when passing through a microburst.

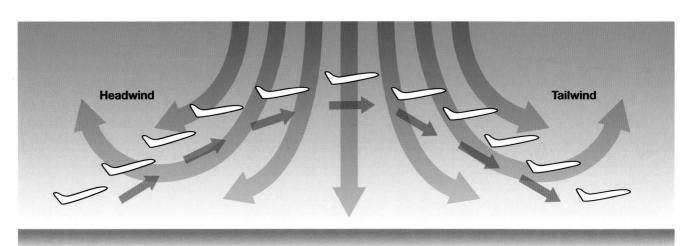

Headwind

Tailwind

sudden **tailwind**—a wind blowing from the tail toward the cockpit. The airflow over the wings then decreases, causing the plane to drop steeply. If the plane is too close to the ground, it may crash. During training, pilots learn how to recognize microbursts and what to do during severe **turbulence.**

Microburst crashes

Since the 1960's, microbursts have caused at least 29 major plane crashes, including the crash of Eastern Airlines Flight 66 on June 24, 1975. The Boeing 727 jet was on its way from New

Orleans, Louisiana, to New York City with 116 passengers and 8 crew members on board. As it approached New York's Kennedy Airport, the plane entered a microburst from a powerful thunderstorm and plummeted downward. It hit the edge of the runway, crashed, and burst into flames, scattering **debris.** Twelve people survived in the rear of the plane, but 112 people died.

Microbursts can also threaten aircraft during takeoff. On July 9, 1982, Pan American World Airways Flight 759 was flying west from Miami to Las Vegas via New Orleans. It landed safely at New Orleans and took off again. But a microburst struck when the plane had risen just 120 feet (36 meters) into the air. The blast of sinking air caused Flight 759 to fall from the sky. It crashed into houses at the end of the runway and exploded in a fireball. All 145 people on board died, along with 8 people on the ground.

Air traffic controllers use Doppler radar technology to monitor the skies for air turbulence and microbursts.

DOPPLER RADAR

In recent years, new technology has enabled flight controllers to pinpoint microbursts and turbulence. One of the most important is a device called Doppler **radar**. This system sends out radar waves that bounce back from rain, **hail,** and powerful **air currents.** Flight controllers can warn pilots of turbulence and, if necessary, delay or reroute flights.

SAFETY IN THUNDERSTORMS

Every year, thunderstorms kill between 100 and 200 people in the United States and injure many others. After being struck by lightning, most victims die from either heart failure or severe burns.

Lightning kills about 20 percent of the people it strikes. About 70 percent of victims suffer such lasting injuries as memory loss, numbness, or muscle spasms. According to some survivors, lightning may also singe, shred, or blast off clothing and blow off people's shoes.

Lightning victims

Most lightning victims are hit while involved in such outdoor activities as hiking or camping. The most dangerous activities include fishing and golfing because metal fishing rods and golf clubs will **conduct** electric current. Lightning victims include the American golfer Lee Trevino, who was hit during a tournament in 1975. Trevino suffered lasting damage to his spine.

A bolt of cloud-to-ground lightning is attracted to the tallest feature in the landscape, in this case a tree.

Safety advice

People can stay safe in a thunderstorm by following a few simple rules. Seek shelter in a house or large building. However, don't use a telephone with a cord, except during an emergency, because electric current from lightning can travel down the telephone wires. If you are caught outdoors, never take shelter under a lone tree. Lightning takes the shortest path to the ground, traveling through tall objects. Stay away from metal objects such as bicycles, and don't use an umbrella. Instead, sit or crouch on the ground.

In addition, be aware that water conducts electricity. If you are swimming, leave the water as quickly as possible. In flat terrain such as a beach, crouch to avoid being the tallest point in the landscape. It is safe to sit in a car, but be sure to close the windows and avoid touching any metal parts.

The metal rod of a lightning conductor lessens the risk of a building being damaged by lightning.

LIGHTNING CONDUCTORS

Lightning conductors protect buildings by channeling electric current safely down to the ground. A metal rod fixed to the tallest part of a building is connected to a long copper wire or cable that runs into the ground. If lightning strikes, electric current passes harmlessly down the cable. In addition, tall buildings protect shorter, neighboring buildings by attracting lightning. For example, the Empire State Building in New York City is struck by lightning about 100 times every year. It has also been struck as many as 15 times in 15 minutes during severe storms.

WINDSTORMS

In the **tropics,** masses of warm, **humid** air feed violent thunderstorms and vast, spinning storms called **hurricanes.** In **temperate** regions, **weather systems** called **cyclones** develop in places where cold air from the **polar** regions collides with warm air from the tropics. Such collisions may produce thunderstorms, **blizzards,** and violent windstorms known as **gales.**

Big blows

Windstorms known as "big blows" typically strike such temperate parts of the United States as the northwest. Severe gales also sweep through northern Europe, particularly during winter. Most European windstorms begin in the North Atlantic Ocean and are blown northeast by winds from the southwest. They generally travel east across northern Scotland toward Norway, affecting relatively unpopulated areas. However, occasionally such storms track farther south, crossing densely populated parts of the United Kingdom, Ireland, France, the Netherlands, Denmark, and Germany.

A severe windstorm with wind speeds of up to 90 miles (145 kilometers) per hour wrecked a solid brick house in Denmark in 1999.

The "Great Storm" of 1703

In November 1703, a severe storm hit southern areas of the United Kingdom. The "Great Storm" raged for a week, flattening trees, destroying thousands of homes, and wrecking ships at sea. Experts believe that about 8,000 people died during one of the worst natural disasters ever recorded in the region.

The Tay Bridge disaster

On Dec. 28, 1879, another severe gale brought disaster to Scotland. In the middle of the night, violent winds wrecked a section of the Tay Bridge, which spans the mouth of the River Tay on Scotland's east coast. The Tay Bridge carries the rail line between Burntisland and Dundee. A train crossing the bridge at the time plunged into the black waters of the river. None of the 75 people on board survived.

IRELAND'S BIG WIND

The night of January 6 to 7, 1839, is known as the "Night of the Big Wind" in Ireland. On that night, a severe windstorm brought winds gusting at hurricane force. The storm killed from 250 to 300 people and destroyed hundreds of thousands of houses.

Waves strike a stationary train on a coastal railroad in southern England during a severe gale in 2004.

The steam locomotive that plunged into the River Tay during the Tay Bridge disaster of 1879 is displayed after it was recovered.

THE NORTH SEA FLOODS OF 1953

Windstorms may produce sudden swells of tidal waves called **storm surges. Gale**-force winds blowing across the sea surface drive the water toward coasts. The low-pressure center at the heart of the storm sucks up water, causing a bulge to form on the sea below it. When a storm surge occurs at the same time as a high **tide,** it can cause flooding on coasts.

The 1953 storm

On Jan. 31, 1953, a severe gale produced a storm surge in the North Sea. The surge caused flooding along the United Kingdom's and the Netherlands' coasts. Like most European storms, this **weather system** originated out in the Atlantic Ocean. The storm headed northeast, sweeping across Ireland and toward Scotland. A ferry, the *Princess Victoria*, sank in the Irish Sea with the loss of 133 lives. The storm raged across northern Scotland and then veered southward around eastern Britain, driving a surge of water before it.

Rising sea levels

The North Sea is relatively shallow between the United Kingdom and western Europe. As the storm surge entered the narrow channel between East Anglia and the Netherlands, sea levels rose by 5 to 10 feet (1.5 to 3 meters). In the early

Floodwaters cover the village of Stellendam in the Netherlands after the storm surge caused by the gale of 1953.

1950's, the United Kingdom had no centralized flood warning system. The storm brought down telephone lines, making it impossible to alert settlements farther south about the floodwaters surging toward them.

The storm surge swept over coastal defenses along the eastern shores of the United Kingdom and the Netherlands. In the United Kingdom, the waters flooded 180,000 acres (72,000 hectares) of land, damaged 24,000 homes, and killed 307 people. In the Netherlands, where much of the land lies below sea level, the storm caused even greater damage. Storm waters flooded 322,500 acres (130,000 hectares) of farm land. Over 46,000 homes were flooded, and 1,835 people drowned.

The gates of the Thames Barrier are in a raised position to prevent floodwaters from swamping London.

THE THAMES BARRIER

The city of London, which lies on the Thames River in southeast England, also suffered damage from the 1953 flood. The storm reached the mouth of the Thames and traveled upriver, flooding docks and factories. In London, it breached river defenses to flood 1,000 homes in the East End area. After the flood, the city built the Thames Barrier to prevent a similar disaster. When a flood warning is issued, the city raises a barrier stretching across the river to protect the city from a storm surge. London completed this flood defense in 1982.

THE GREAT GALE OF 1987

On Oct. 15 to 16, 1987, a severe storm hit northwest Europe. Northern France and southern England experienced the most intense effects of this **gale.** People did not expect such a strong storm because severe windstorms rarely sweep so far south.

Unexpected weather

The Great Gale of 1987 began on the afternoon of October 15 as a weak **cyclone** over the Bay of Biscay, off the coasts of France and Spain. At first, **meteorologists** did not forecast a severe storm. However, the cyclone gained strength from unusually warm air in the Bay of Biscay. It may also have combined with very strong winds carried across the Atlantic Ocean from **Hurricane** Floyd, which had raged across Florida in the United States a few days earlier. By 6:00 p.m., the storm had grown and was heading north. However, British meteorologists did not predict a severe gale until 1:30 a.m. on the morning of October 16, when most people were asleep. As a result, few were prepared.

The Great Gale of 1987 roars past southern England in this false-color satellite image.

Early on October 16, the storm struck northern France, flattening crops and wrecking houses. Four people died, and millions of trees were uprooted. The gale then veered north to Cornwall, on England's southwest tip. Winds gusting at more than 60 miles (100 kilometers) per hour battered England's south coast, sending trees smashing onto cars, homes, roads, and railroad tracks. Southeast England bore the brunt of the storm. The gale killed 16 people, damaged thousands of homes, and left 7 million homes without electricity.

Trees in southern Britain lay toppled by the Great Gale of 1987.

COMPARING STORMS

People often compare the Great Gale of 1987 to the Great Storm of 1703 (see page 39). Historians think that the 1703 storm killed 8,000 people—far more than died in the 1987 gale. However, because trees and buildings in southern England are not normally exposed to such high winds, the 1987 gale caused massive destruction. It uprooted 15 million trees and damaged thousands of structures.

ACTIVITY

Thunder and lightning provide a spectacular display of nature's power. People find it interesting to observe a thunderstorm from a safe place indoors. You could record your observations about storms and other wild weather in a weather diary. Write down the types of lightning you see, including forked, streak, or sheet lightning. Also note the sounds of thunder, from distant rumbles to loud claps.

Measuring the distance to a storm

Light travels much faster than sound. This means that you see lightning at nearly the same instant that it strikes, but the sound of thunder takes longer to reach you. You can use this fact to measure the distance between you and a storm.

Equipment

- Pen and paper
- Optional: watch, clock, or stopwatch that shows seconds

1. Get your equipment ready as the storm approaches. When you see lightning flash, begin to count the seconds. If you have a watch, clock, or stopwatch that shows seconds, you can use it to measure the seconds more accurately.
2. Stop counting as soon as you hear the thunder. Write down the number of seconds between the lightning and the thunder.
3. Sound takes about 5 seconds to cover 1 mile (about 3 seconds to cover 1 kilometer). Divide the number of seconds you counted by 5 (or 3 if using kilometers) to find out the distance to the storm.
4. Repeat steps 1 to 3 as lightning strikes again. Is the storm moving closer or farther away? If the storm is more than 15 miles (24 kilometers) away, you probably won't hear the thunder.

air current A flow of air in a particular direction.

air mass A body of air at a particular temperature, humidity, and height.

atmosphere The layer of gases surrounding Earth.

atmospheric pressure The weight of the air pressing down on Earth's surface.

atom The smallest particle of a chemical element.

blizzard A heavy snowstorm with high winds.

canyon A narrow rift in the land with high, steep sides.

charge separation The separation of positive and negative electrically charged particles in a thundercloud that causes lightning to spark.

cloudburst A sudden, intense rainfall over a small area.

condense To change from a gas to a liquid as a result of cooling.

conduct To carry electric current.

cumulonimbus cloud A massive, vertical cloud formation, often with a flat top.

cyclone A violent, swirling windstorm or the weather systems in which these windstorms form.

debris Rubble, broken objects, and other damaged material.

derecho A storm with violent winds that blow in one direction.

discharge To release.

downdraft A downward movement of air.

drought A long period of unusually dry weather.

electrical Related to electricity.

electron A tiny, negatively charged particle.

equator An imaginary line around the middle of Earth, halfway between the North and South poles.

evaporate To change from a liquid into vapor.

eye The calm area at the center of a hurricane.

firebreak Land cleared of fuel to stop or slow the progress of a fire.

flash flood A sudden, intense flood of a river or lake.

freezing point The temperature at which a liquid freezes.

front In weather, the place where two masses of air meet.

gale A very strong wind; technically, any wind with a velocity of 32 to 63 miles (51 to 101 kilometers) per hour.

gorges Deep, narrow valleys, usually steep and rocky, especially ones with a stream.

hail Rounded or irregularly shaped pellets of ice that may fall from thunderclouds.

hail embryo A frozen raindrop or snow pellet from which a hailstone develops.

headwind A wind blowing toward the front of such objects as airplanes.

humid Describes moist air.

hurricane A tropical storm over the North Atlantic Ocean, the Caribbean Sea, the Gulf of Mexico, or the Northeast Pacific Ocean.

ice meteor An unusually large chunk of ice that falls from the sky.

landslide A mass of soil and rock that slides down a slope.

leader A channel of electric charge going from a thundercloud toward the ground or from the ground toward a thundercloud.

lightning conductor A device or material that conducts electric current from lightning.

mesocyclone A rotating column of air that forms inside a thundercloud and can produce tornadoes.

meteorologist A scientist who studies and forecasts the weather.

microburst A localized flow of rapidly sinking air.

polar Describes the regions around the North and South poles.

radar An electronic device that allows weather forecasters to locate areas of rain or snow and track the motion of air in weather systems.

radiation Energy given off in the form of waves or small particles.

St. Elmo's fire A form of lightning that appears as a ghostly glow sometimes seen around tall, pointed objects during thunderstorms.

shock wave A violent vibration in air sometimes caused by the rapid expansion of the air.

squall A sudden rise in the wind.

squall line A line of thunderclouds produced during a squall.

storm surge A rapid rise in sea level produced when winds drive ocean waters ashore.

stroke An upward-moving spark going from the ground to a thundercloud.

supercell A powerful, long-lasting thunderstorm that often produces heavy rain, hail, and tornadoes.

supercooled Describes a liquid that has cooled to below its normal freezing point without freezing.

tailwind A wind blowing toward the back of such objects as airplanes.

temperate Describes the regions between the tropics and the polar regions.

tide The regular rise and fall in sea levels on coasts.

tornado A whirling funnel of high-speed winds that stretches from a thundercloud to the ground.

tornado outbreak A group of tornadoes that form within a short time.

tropics Regions of Earth that lie within about 1,600 miles (2,570 kilometers) north and south of the equator.

turbulence A disturbance in the air, caused by winds such as updrafts and downdrafts.

updraft An upward movement of air.

water vapor Water in the form of a gas.

weather system A particular set of weather conditions in Earth's atmosphere, which affects a certain area or region for a period of time.

wind shear A sudden change of wind speed or direction that occurs over a short distance.

BOOKS

Disaster! Weather, by Jen Green, Belitha Press, 2002.

Extreme Weather, by Terry Jennings, Evans Brothers, 2005.

Repairing the Damage: Hurricanes and Storms, by Clint Twist, Evans Brothers, 1997.

Eyewitness Natural Disasters, by Claire Watts, Dorling Kindersley, 2006.

What on Earth? Lightning, by Brian Williams, Book House, 2005.

WEB SITES

http://thirteen.org/savageplanet/03deadlyskies/01lforms/indexmid.html

http://thunder.msfc.nasa.gov/primer/index.html

http://www.fema.gov/hazard/thunderstorm/index.shtm

http://www.yellowstone-bearman.com/yfire.html

http://www.spc.noaa.gov/misc/AbtDerechos/derechofacts.htm

INDEX